# Blending Colors

# Blending Colors

Poems

Jeffrey L. Johnson

RESOURCE *Publications* • Eugene, Oregon

BLENDING COLORS
Poems



Resource Publications
An Imprint of Wipf and Stock Publishers
199 W. 8th Ave., Suite 3
Eugene, OR 97401

www.wipfandstock.com

PAPERBACK ISBN: 979-8-3852-7348-5
HARDCOVER ISBN: 979-8-3852-7349-2
EBOOK ISBN: 979-8-3852-7350-8

VERSION NUMBER 04/02/26

*Cezanne's extreme concentration breaks through into a feeling as carefree and unencumbered as that which surrounds us in nature itself.*

—John Updike

*We make out of the quarrel with others, rhetoric,*
*but of the quarrel with ourselves, poetry.*

—William Butler Yeats

*Look at the birds.*

—Jesus, son of Mary

## Contents

## Lost Today

socks in driers
cellphones in Ubers
names of neighbors' kids
golf balls in long rough
baseballs in gardens
eyeglasses in waiting rooms
desire for another drink
in evening souls
warmed enough by one
virginity
belief in the holy trinity
childhood friendships
faith in democracy
trust in government
caps of pens
songbirds in branches
careless, child-like confidence
in the gain of adolescence
board games
lawsuits
bets at roulette wheels
chances at love
opportunities to travel

will to succeed
car keys
parking places on the street
dogs roaming widely
cats prowling in the dark
one hundred kinds
of insects.

## Auditions of the Birds

When you woke this morning
with a song held over from a dream,
beginning and intermediate vocalizers
outside heard it and in fledgling
outreach noted their backgrounds
and preparations as warblers, trillers,
chirpers, croakers, and screechers.

Birds of a feather appeared from afar,
asking for guidance and for seeds.
Inquiring owls advanced partnership
proposals from prominent branches.
A murmuration of starlings landed,
hoping for advice in assembling
with better blending as a robed choir.

There were badass bands of punk crows,
comic huckles of sparrows, folk
quartets of turkeys, choruses of Canada
geese, formal in attire and arrangement,
tuning for their rehearsal overhead.

## Hitchhiker

At a crossroads, when you slow down,
look right and notice that god bailed out,
without a nod, from the passenger seat.

If memories of god remain as you drive,
they will combine and dissipate
in the evening's orange and purple.

In the morning, song birds will wake
to dance with angels in the arms of trees.
Gambols like theirs have been imitated,

the sounds recorded, transcribed, shelved
and forgotten by all but pale souls who sort
and store silent stacks of yesterday's signs.

In the morning, out of confusion or sleep
deprivation, you might pull off the road,
lean over, and motion for god to sit in again.

Driving with god beats wondering where
god went—and why—and whether god,
gone so long, no longer exists.

With god next to you, clouds mingle.
Nervous dogs feel safe with strangers.
Emergency faith is stowed to make room

for god the pauper, prostitute, beggar,
orphan, hobo, and hitchhiker to appear to
restore seasons, arid and moist, to tease

revelations, bless farewells and greetings,
supply insight for soul doctors to proclaim
without having to say in public presentations

what they admit to themselves in private
moments, that apathy and cruelty infect
the heart with variations of the same pain.

## Night Moves in Rome

The night Cézanne died in the rain
the Pope was still amassing art

and graven images of marble,
lining them up in Vatican hallways.

How much hoarding would satisfy
the Pope before he would end all

the laying up and heaping, and begin
restoring treasures to earth's ends?

Statues, frozen in perfection, sullen
in closeted imprisonment, stirred

from their stiffness after midnight.
Miles away from Rome, Cézanne

boomed through a village, bent
forward on the handlebars of a

motorcycle on a roar for a comely
riding partner or for a friendly face

to notice him blasting above cobbles,
haunting without an aim in a riff

so loud it rippled bedroom curtains
and shivered cups on saucers.

## Trinity

If your god is an idyll,
let fair weather and storms
draw your heart to praise.

On a walk early, or in the cool
of an evening, speak softly.
Your god is omnipresent.

If you know your god's name,
call it out loudly, as if your god
is a friend. Don't be disappointed

if your god does not answer.
Gods with known names are busy.
Your god is omniscient.

If your god's name is a secret,
unspoken even by the priests,
your god is holy. Be careful.

Namelessness erases doubt.
Nothing contains everything.
Your god is omnipotent.

## Spring Break

Shine on, Carolinas, hanging out
down there, looking east-
southeast. You're the cool kids.

You walk the dogs, lead the pack,
set the pace, share the weed.
Share the love, Carolinas!

Let fermentation flow to block
news that a committee
of elders approved a resolution

declaring that rules of war
were violated in a butchery
far away, beside another sea.

Your rules are set by margins
of ocean and sand,
by petitions of waves in their

tumblings and scrubbings.
Keep the sea shining where it tucks
in at your beaches and bays,

shimmered by the moon
in the evening and unshy in
alliance with the morning sun.

## My I Come In?

Woes travel winding ways.
The wend today was a spiral
of languages and locations.

Excuse me. The door was unlocked,
so I came in.
French is my first language.

I drove down from New Hampshire
to look for a friend who lives
in how do you say it? Around here.

I should tell you that
when I was young, I was afraid
of everything, nervous all day

until I was stung by yellowjackets.
The bees took my brain.
Then a little girl got it back for me.

We lived together in Connecticut,
then in New Hampshire.
Then I hit my head. Long story.

Landed in the ER, all alone until
she turned me around and took
my brain home with her again.

Later I lost my house. Long story.
You don't want to hear it.
I get turned around all the time.

My friend is out this way.
I can't say the name of the town.
I could use money for gas.

## Evidence

A strong wind might take a big branch
without warning or comment.
The wind plays rough with old trees.

The gods play rough too. They keep trysts
and affairs and hold collegial conclaves
to mediate matters beyond their control.

I intend to invoke the gods to sit together
on the dread I have done, a sorry stump
of a great white pine that towered even

when Thoreau rambled by, when white-
bearded Longfellow bellowed in rhyme.
Its needles scratched the arms

of the wind and chopped sunlight to dapples
on the ground. The gods and old poets
together might absolve me of my misdeed.

They have time to trace the packed rounds
of the trunk, an abstract archive of seasons,
some preserving years of rain that satisfied

reaching roots, others narrow of drought
years when young twigs, ready for go-
arounds with the wind, cracked and fell.

## Icon

It’s your birthday, you solid-as-a-rock star.
Enjoy it out there, nowhere without end.

You may have noticed our decline.
Private pics are shared for likes and loves.

Video shorts try to go viral, like the tale of the
shepherd you heard of who found his sheep

safe and asleep, or the one about a woman
who turned her house inside out to find a coin.

We search for heroes in wild-goose chases
through podcasts and blogs, hoping to land on

an essential face like yours, a face held in place
firmly within a frame wide enough to keep

meaning from spilling out, deep enough to hold
hope in reserve below shoulders square

and motionless in ancestral stillness, eyes
pillowed in peace, oblivious to the wages of sin.

## Conclave

Luna's back and forth efforts resulted
in hell and high water on earth,
so Apollo announced a new creation.

Hermes, fluent in the planet's dialects,
spoke quietly to desert introspectives,
raised his voice to mountain knights,

woke stern prairie aunts from naps, called
cold-forest princes and rainforest cousins
to attention, convened rivers and water-

ways to increase their floods forward to
the four ocean queens in petition that
that they might turn as one vapor

to the stars that keep the formula for
the original mixture of mysticism and
matter, and ask them to pour it out again.

## Rumor

We could use a real jaw-dropper,
a holy-cow shocker to help us
forget about Washington
and the weather.

I mean the coming out
of a relative or an out-of-the-blue
affair between parents we know,
a diagnosis to stop time,

a flabbergaster unearthed
from a basement file cabinet
or spilled like a flood of tears
from a storage box on moving day.

We have no further need for
for yawns of open secrets, the kind
that are repeated, ignored,
or forgotten, like yesterday's lunch,

such as that faith is affection,
love is mainly patience,
and discipline is the heart's peace.

## Night Moves in Paris

*We were like those who dream.*

Prepared to take us back a century,
our wobbling guide drew attention

to something plain: a mound of life
and wool on a patch of grass in front

of the café from which her literary
tour was to begin, a breathing heap

under street dust sprayed from cars
and shoes misted in Left Bank dew.

"He's been there three days. It's still
a little seedy around here. You can see."

Not seedy. Seeded. Seeded with dreams,
like the one I wished for that three-day

sleeper, wrapped in a cocoon of wool
and plastic. I wished for him

a midnight beach dream of a raven-
haired woman under the moon and stars

aware of pearls on her neck and an orchid
in her hair. Walking, we caught up with

and recalled other dreamers alone
at typewriters in rented garrets the size

of closets, and together in Gertrude Stein's
parlor, getting drunk on absinthe.

The Latin Quarter was a bunkhouse
with Ezra Pound, the punk rooster, strutting

and crowing, and Hemingway dreaming
of Michigan lakes, and Fitzgerald thinking

up ways to leave Zelda, and Joyce anxious
to find a publisher for his cure for insomnia.

## Shadows

A commuter, hyperbolizing pop songs
from his car's radio, palming beats
against the steering wheel.

A daydreamer, reviewing names
for a dog she will never own, aware
that a normal dog name would save

her the awkwardness of explaining
the origin of an unusual one in answer
to a question that will never be asked.

A man alone in his room with all
that remains and someone else's
television on the wall. Young

women in and out never stay long
enough to brighten days he feels
as a melting out of measure

and authority into an elastic eternity.
A woman, aware that she cannot keep
dreams because she is no longer young.

## Custody

Count on instrumentalists
to produce sure sounds.
Directors dance alone.

Gyrating and gesturing,
keeping heaven and earth,
players and patrons, together.

Pity the maestros, leaders
of ensembles, captive servant-
captains without freedom

to run from ice cream windows
to the backseats of family SUVs,
forced to forget that an alley

sheltered by a wall is best
for galloping and that a footpath
winding through an attentive

audience of trees is good for
skipping to the beat of a tune
from the back of their minds.

## Incense

I have little to say, but I have breath
to call upon my neighbor and to call
upon god in the draft of the holy spirit.

I call upon my neighbor for a ride
to the airport. I call upon god in prayer.
Even silent prayer is not breathless.

The substance of prayer is smoke,
not sound, so light it up, deacon,
swing the censer like you mean it.

Tick tock, tick tock, taking us out of time
in spirits that dance then disappear.
Let not our breath be timed with that

of those who assemble in greed.
Let our breath be matched to righteous
and experienced drivers like my father,

a priest of fishing. He held the steering
wheel of our *Pontiac* station wagon
between his knees when he lit cigars.

*Dutch Masters* smoke filtered through
my mother's puffed hairdos. Then evil-
doers had no place on our pilgrimages.

## Drifter

Europeans thought they brought
Jesus to the Indians, but Jesus was
a brother the Indians already knew.

Jesus never fussed at smudgy fires
or rusty door panels, never noticed
wounded siding or bruised backyards.

If an Indian father was not available
to his child he might allow her
to be given to Jesus, because Jesus

had a way of learning a child's every
weakness even when the child
did not yet know her own mind.

Jesus held children in his arms,
this we know, and never felt a heart-
deep need to run off somewhere.

Jesus was always ready for a car ride.
He would hop in, passenger side
or back seat, and listen carefully

all the way, without saying a word.
Jesus stopped by church every week
but never stayed more than an hour.

Outdoors, Jesus walked side by side
on late-night rambles, keeping Indian
hearts near the Great Spirit's heart.

When Europeans took Jesus back,
he relearned their ways and looked
to the Indians like a chief enchained.

## Still Life

It has been imagined
that ghosts come and go
as embodied spirits do,
but it should not be thought
that ghosts move through
time and space the way we
normally think of moving.

Ghosts I have known feel
welcome in low lights,
when champagne is flat,
when wires are crossed.
Ghosts like it when they
recline, free of form, in
blue, and motionless.

## Sanctums

Some school buildings were built
in shame and sorrow. A shame
is that from sunrise to sunset
we lock our children up in them.

Soon after they learn to walk
we teach them to march in order.
Some days they emerge under the sun
like inmates released for a breath of air.

A sorrow is that a hill, good
for sledding, was shaved smooth
for an asphalt lot with solar panels,
mantis-like, straddling parked cars.

Hard edges keep soft bodies quiet.
Earth was created in love and mercy.
If only school buildings, like mountains
and valleys, could testify to grace.

Hills look like they were molded
by toddlers, trees in the woods wave
arms in the wind like children do
before they are told to keep still.

Birds, fluent in languages, write essays
in the sky and sign them in songs.

## Giving Tanks

Where is the Lord praised in the evening?
In the chipmunk's burrow, under the shed.
In the curl of the fox's body, buried in sleep.
Before first light the fox will trot rounds
beside the stream for mice in the grass,
through backyards for a quail at the feeder,
in the garden for a cottontail, too slow.

Where is a room with quiet words, peaceful
blessings pressed down on sleeping brows?
Where is prayer in the body's twilight?
Where, in what archive of mind, is a voice
recorded telling children to notice glitter
tints of tropical fish sold on the side
by a couple who carded and bundled wool?

Words that invited toddlers in tow to try
praising floating brightness of kissing
gouramis, barbs, tetras, mollies and guppies,
lose themselves in endorsement of liquid
enchantment in bubbles rising behind glass
while backing the purpose of a shy pair
making ends meet with an unlikely hustle.

## Saxonville

*They do not fear the spirits*
*too much to feel an artistic*
*and humorous pleasure.*
—W.B. Yeats

Seeing, they perceive not,
hearing, they understand not
is not true of these neighbors.
They seem to see clearly,
hear without distortion.

If it is right to say they exist,
then they exist beyond the fringe
of space, free from slippages
of time and gaps of knowledge.
Sometimes they decide to trail us

with a wangle or mischief
such as arranging for Christmas
lights to stay on out of season,
stretched with Happy New Year
across a bungalow window,

a sight that stirs up a seepage of
festive feelings sealed for months
already in a driver stopped
in encouraging brightness and
warmth on the first day of spring.

## Vernal Song

*We are reformers*
*in the spring and summer.*
—Ralph Waldo Emerson

A simple cure for the heartache
of homesickness is homelessness.

High and mighty are stars above.
Wise and waiting is soil somewhere.

For distant stars to sing something
or for shy and gifted soil to shout

out loud in colors and finishes
requires visions of a seer, or seeds

with amendments pressed in by hand,
or research into ignorance, or prayers

submitted in silence to gray history
and purple sadness Sunday morning.

## Retreat

If you ever meet a bear on a trail,
move away slowly from the bear.

Skate backward. Moonwalk.
Take your time. Melt into the woods

where you belong, with the trees,
rooted in syllables of sound and light

your ancestors knew as breath in leaves
and light sifted across the forest floor.

Your ancestors measured moisture
in the soil through their bare feet.

The trees will tell you in peace
that bears keep no schedules.

They have no plans, nothing going on
other than more sniggers under rocks,

snuffles into crumbling logs, snorts
without envy along a shoreline,

galumphings in shallow water without
goals. So take it easy. Redirect yourself

calmly. Go back where you can be
yourself again, at ease, hidden and free.

## Becoming an Adjective

Grief in a lonely station falls thick
and sweet like maple syrup,
faint and clean like pressed sheets,

rich in thought like chocolate,
dismal in the throat like a bite
of a *Cotton Candy* crayon.

Too bad the squirrels aren't around.
They're asleep, heads under tails,
at rest from a day of stitching loops

to keep dismay tucked away
under the sod, out of sight.
Squirrels mend rifted relationships,

suture fissures of diplomacy, stop
hope from bleeding out by bouncing
from mishap to emergency.

They spring from bruise to fracture
to laceration, stop in a freeze,
look around for trouble then drop

down a medicinal nut and brush
on an analgesic with swipes
of preponderant tails.

In the morning they'll wake and try
daring, tail-twirling darts again,
dashing as if judged for difficulty

and speed from branches above.
When two cars meet with a scrambler
between them, the peril is high

for that go-getter, out there trying
to cover a strip of asphalt, hauling
nuts like nouns haul adjectives.

## Scattered

When the sun idles in autumn,
and the party dies in the west,
crows badger the sun.
They clown-hop and mock
the sun for being lazy and slow.

An owl screeches for a mate
to take away the pain.
Sometime short of noon
shorebirds explore stained sand.
Horseflies go for blood.

High-flying cormorants look
for backwaters where they can
land, unfold and stretch.
Clouds pass overhead like waves.
Waves break over the sand.

Before he told a secret held
hard in his heart, the sun melted
his shame to insignificant regret.

Sparrows held a reception.
Squirrels chased doves.
Jays flapped at squirrels.
Chipmunks ministered in grain
under a backyard pole of life.

## Pilgrim Moon

At the well-known hour, cool came down,
veiled in thickness, draped in shadows.

Birds and small animals tucked into
evening secrets early.

Dreams called by the what of the hour
peered out through window blinds.

Premature and unformed, they faded
when trinkets and bangles jangled

to become reminders of a rarity in the sky,
a once or twice in a lifetime moon-curse

of foolishness, with homage to the still
enthroned, imperial, reappearing sun.

## Easter Afternoon

Weeding perennials, I uncovered
god under a mat of last year's mulch.

Resting and helping might be one
and the same for god.

Even though I knelt on the earth with
god, I did not fret my sinfulness,

and god did not judge or indulge
my neglectful gardening with grace,

even though god surely could tell
that my efforts were unclever.

Down in the root systems, god might
have been relaxing, on retreat from

providence or from resting for an eon
before working through all that was,

all that is, and all that is to come.
Laying a blessing on god with a full

shovel, I excused myself to scrape
the crumbles of time a while longer.

## Fishing from a Bridge

Their days begin at mid-morning
and end before the sun and the clerks

have gone back to their places.
The men are small and brown,

without caps and without leisure.
Their shaded stations are spaced

for thoughts to stay private, close
enough for spirits to stay juiced

by jokes called across tangles in
a jetsam of immigrant languages.

Barbs cast between the men splash
as they imitate the kind of work

that might feed their families.
Incurious, the river keeps its only

schedule, indulging the fishermen's
angling for their fathers' routines.

Shoppers duck in and out of stores
behind them. Cars cruise by smoothly.

## Genealogies

A sentimental homebody with
ancestors arranged in an album

might know that this one was mother
of that one and that one was father

of twins in a town on the river, over
a dry sea, down a grove-guarded drive.

One by one we lift off, each of us
a sign of something, an example,

a model, hope for resolution, a dream
thrown out the window, tangled

in thistles and cockleburs, covered
in dust of a lonely gravel road.

Will your grandchildren's children
know your baptismal name?

The vanished are recalled in reviews
trimmed, with pleasures scrubbed

to mildest virtues dressed soberly
to keep the wordcount down.

## Gone-Away Feelings

Leaded glass veiled in lace within
a walnut frame ajar enough to show

a strip of china cabinet and a sliver
of mirror suggesting useful things

displayed for occasions when time
pretends to admire what was

bequeathed or left behind, tokens
reminding how it ends in gone-away.

Finery resolves to kitsch and kitsch
settles to recyclables and leavings.

## Quotidian

Curse, and your kids will be
accursed by your spells.

Find a way to get high,
and you might feel the sublimity

of a constellation or the cacophony
of coral in a jumble under the tide.

Straighten up and fly right into
the face of every headwind.

She never wore a cross or any
other identifying jewelry

when she dropped anchor
in still water, one in a flotilla

(I'm guessing) of quiet children
in the narrows of a shallow bay.

I waited on the near shore, always
unprepared to see a young face,

a beloved face, a promising face,
facing facts without regret or fear.

## Think of Me

I used to think of you a lot.
Now that you have gone away
I have you to myself.

A story told is a story changed.
A memory held between us
is a moment kept.

You crossed over every day
after bran cereal, orange juice,
and coffee taken alone.

An only child, you faced up
happily to distant blood claims
and visits from strangers.

From your recliner you stitched
patterns to splice in threads
of neighbors' stories.

Your love, unreserved, your
interest in others, respectful
and alert, cleared the room

for their voices. But even
the strongest singers, trained
in attention, like you were,

cannot carry us home, so we
have refrains: I needed you
more than you needed me.

## Good Dog Too

Our cancers are similar,
scientists say. The materials

of our tumors arrive
dissolved in blood then

are assembled in mystery
while we play fetch or swim

in the lake together.
Sit and stay.

Night is falling for both of us.
You sleep outdoors, curl

your short years in a corner,
away from my touch.

Good dog. That's a good dog.
Sleeping arrangements

are complicated. I am
a good dog too. I sit and stay.

## Every Gift is Placed

Good things come
to those who no longer care,

to those who correspond
with ancient crackpots
and fools of old,

to those who speak quietly
to a silent father rumored
to be listening,

to those who know a mother
unfamiliar with worry,
unchanged by the seasons,

to those who pay full,
un-ticketed attention
to the leaves of three lilacs,

two dogwoods, and the wings
of a flicker at a feeder,
leader of a flutter-chorus

directed by the west wind
in close collaboration
with the evening sun.

## Sara Smiled

*Smile awhile for me, Sara.*

—Hall and Oates

Fat cross the face, Sara rubbed
against my leg when I walked
into my best friend's kitchen.
I never spent time with Sara
apart from those matronly
approaches and leg-rub hellos
until last night when she
appeared, crossing a threshold,
cat-walking down the narrow
hallway of a dream. Remember
me, Sara? I thought you smiled.

## Miserable Month

Work over April with questions.
Don't let the month get away
without a thorough grilling.

Look for a quiet place for straight
talk with that trickster, April, so
smug, smiling and crying at will.

For a quiet place, try a wide prairie,
a beach, or a sky view. These three
faraways won't interrupt you.

Wide places like these welcome
listeners, but they are not listening
in. They are hosts for listeners.

Wide places are ministers of nothing,
not even of silence. They call flocks
to temples of nowhere.

Still they vibrate distinct tones
and intensities, bypassing ears
and entering certain souls, feeding

native birds with pitches like seeds
that the birds transpose
to songs they use for survival.

Look long enough into a wide place
and loneliness will move in on you
like sunshine and storm, move over

and around you, like April, without
a settled story. Hear the month out,
then let May turn the page.

## Aubade

If you show me the door,
I'll show you salvation.

We'll turn on a dime
and lean on each other

to keep our balance.
You prefer sunflowers

in the wind to roses
in crystal. We have

common ground there.
Shaggy-head flowers

feed birds and stand high
and unsteady for more

than an indoor fling in cut
glass and fancy pants.

When I was a fool
for you, frost was on

the pumpkin, a dish ran
away with a spoon,

violets sported new blue,
horses finally got sense.

## Cabernet and Mayonnaise

A recognition of extractions,
preparations and products

to smooth glides, grease gears,
massage bearings, calm nerves,

soothe souls. Paraffin, lanolin,
beeswax, hooch passed around,

grease guns, graphite rubs, WD-40,
courtesies on trains, bouquets

at the door, candy wrapped
in ribbons, glycerin, aloe vera,

olive oil, candelilla oil, coconut oil,
canola oil, gravy, butter, schmaltz,

smears, spreads, preserves, bacon
grease, castor oil, lard, egg whites,

meditation, rumination, prayer,
soybean oil, sunflower oil,

safflower oil, rivers of petroleum
bases, laxatives, lecithin, polite

phrases and oozes with varied
purposes and applications.

## Blending Colors with Ancestors

Grandma rode broncos in the rodeo.
Yippee kay-ay kay-oh!

She raced around barrels, roped calves,
and wrestled steers with the cowboys.

Ladies and gentlemen, Grandpa
was a circus clown. He stumbled

and flummoxed under spotlights with
a red nose, yellow shoes and orange hair.

Grandma and Grandpa used to agree
that purple is hard to pin down.

On one hand it's the warm sunset.
On the other hand it's cool and royal.

Where will fun come from now that
the rodeo and the circus have loaded

their beasts, collapsed the marquees,
shaken dust from their spectacles?

## Blending Colors with Strangers

I ask airport strangers to share snacks
with me, but they seem anxious.
Some seem wounded and suspicious.

I would like to tell one of them about
my mother. She was a watcher at the river
until she became one with the river.

You cannot go home again means no one
waits for you, so do whatever you please,
with a visitor's smile that tries to connect

with passersby looking for their children.
Who can say that their own fathers
are not out there searching like forgotten

captains sailing alone over wind-dried
seas in homes splintered by the years
into facets of amethyst and scintillas

of emotion that angle and scatter
in glitter showers of the full spectrum?

## Blending Colors with Children

A woodchuck bumbles out from
snarled underbrush, blinks into
starburst charges of yellow, red,

purple and blue, swings summer
blubber around on a dime and dives
back into intertwisted foliage

it calls home to recover from
the sight and to resume rummaging,
safely separated from a guardian

maple's children side-by-side
at work on overturned plastic pails,
splashing rainbows on white

T-shirts, spangling dollhouses
with dollops of primary colors,
practicing neighborly tones of voice.

## Watchers

Who were you singing for
those Easter mornings, eyes on your
nose in the shaving mirror?

I never imagined you sang for me,
but spirits spill and spread from songs.
No one sings alone.

I believe you sang for the one whose
scant good words made you sing
loudly, so she might hear you.

You are on light duty for me, riding
in on refrains from old crooners,
in hymns, dimly in NFL film clips.

In extremis you are no longer mine.
My attendants are sent from the pool,
next in line, sometimes old dogs.

Once I got an Afro woman. Didn't
recognize her. Middle age, unanxious,
still and aware, until she wasn't there.

## What is the Child's Name?

Tiny hands fisted near her heart,
a brand-new mother touched
the arm of a bedside nurse.
"What's a good name?
I can't think of a name."

The newborn's skin shed names
like it would slough time and events
when it had a name.

Then a playact came to mind.
The mother would pose, look down
into a plastic basin of water
reflecting her own face
and her baby's swaddled body.

A name would arise from the water
when the baby's life was held
in a pantomime.

The mother began, "When the baby's
name is known, will it be written
in the Lamb's book of life?

Do you promise to bring the child
to a holy house, if you find one,
so the child might in time learn
the names of Moses and Jesus,
of Martha and Mary?

Will you emboss the name
in gold on the cover of a bible
to keep the devil outside the circle?
The devil is not good with names.

When the baby has a name, will you
keep it safe, and tell it around,
and recall that it is known forever,
frustrating the forgetful devil."

## Homecoming

Instead of trying to say everything,
be satisfied with having something to say.

Don't be ashamed of scars you bear
from small mistakes.

The prairie is a sea. How much of it
will be swallowed by the wind?

You will not recognize your children
when they are grown. You did not

know them when they were young.
The mother is a river who said goodbye

with blunt affection: "The next time
you visit me, I might not be here."

Look for more than wind-bent grass.
Look for a red bird on a white church,

on a church bleached by the sun,
or look for a hill with barrels rolling

down the face of it like a dream, shaggy
and strange even on their native range.

## Why are You Weeping?

I have a question.
I having nothing but questions.
I ask them again and again
in the same vein.

Why are you crying?
Who are you looking for?
Where have you been?

My questions are not coy,
accusatory or cruel. My
questions provoke sunrises.

I interrogate sleeping buds,
arouse them from branches
brown as tinder for funeral fires.

My questions wake seed pods
from the doze of winter.
What are you waiting for?

What will you be when you
come out of your tomb
in full shape and color?

Mary and Mary Magdalene
sing questions like the desert
sky sings stars.

What do you want?
Where are you going?
Who's going with you?

Mary's heart is a well
of questions. She keeps them all
and turns them from syntaxes

of perplexity to notations
of direction for souls that have
been turned inside out.

Magdalene is an ocean.
Her questions break in
even on her tears.

## Terra Firma

Sleep well at home. The word breathes
warm and steady around and within you,
blessing without ending.

All that was, is and will be, is a word
on the breath of love, inciting rumors
and explanations without exhibition

or remainders in arks and sanctuaries.
Saint Peter's, Chartres, the Blue Mother's
womb. The word pools, swirls, eddies,

circles from an empty tomb to empty
churches, empty wallets, empty hearts.
Blessed are the poor and the dying

and the resplendent lilies of the field,
pouring themselves out in the richness
they have been given, and have to give.

***Lost in wonder, love, and praise.***

—Charles Wesley

When the trumpet of the Lord shall sound,
time shall be no more. Along with time shall go
measures of distance, images of presence,

increments of weight and volume. Shelters
of stone and reputation shall crumble, releasing
prisoners to freedom of being neither lost

nor found, neither in place nor out of place.
Life's partnership with the world shall end, not
according to law and judgment, but according

to law and all ever contained in time and space,
along with all ever known and unknown,
all words invented and forgotten, wrapped

in the word that called out all that would be seen
and unseen. All shall be claimed and saved
from what might have turned out better.

Then shall appear notations: pain forgotten,
mercy spread extravagantly, forgiveness engulfing
shame in fire, guilt immersed in floods within

the dream souls need to dim in devotion
to such as the sea's water and waves, to the still
water in prayer, with the waves in their praise.

## Do Not Be Conformed

Molded, rotating, perfect in orbit
within a flaming soul, the brain
is a seed of everything good.

The soul is heaven, embodied
vessel of all-and-forever, being in
but not belonging to time. Amen.

Earth is the nursery. Fire is the sitter.
Born of earth's tenderness,
tutored to the sun, you are formed.

Do not be conformed by temporal
wounds, muddied by the meltings
of life, chilled by its loneliness.

Try to stay unstained by time's
remainders and the body's vexations.
Decline inquiries of wherefore

and why, of origin and ends.
The Lord is on the wind and away.
Pray for a breeze and spring rain.

## Lost Art

If you cannot read your own handwriting,
you have a spiritual problem on your hands.
In your hand, in your writing hand.

Neatness counts, and I used to try, but third
grade was long ago when Mrs. Posz showed
us tornado swirls, circular and conical as

funnel clouds passing over the prairie,
training us toward graceful penmanship.
My twisters broke apart to scribbles without

form, no thrilling spirals or admirable
curves to show that an impatient boy-hand
had finally gotten the hang of the gyration.

## Summer Devotions

Wander close to a shore bird's nest
and the mother bird might abandon it.
Uninvited visitors bring intrusive vibes
to vulnerable fledglings in the nursery.

Innocence and maturity might combine
to produce courage and mercy
that overcomes ignorance and dispels
the fear of being alone in the woods

with imagination as your companion.
A community in its plurality needs
the fulness of firm and full solitary
souls to shape it from within.

Tomatoes hold sacraments of water
and seeds in a religion of earth-flesh,
fiber, and juice jeweled out in ruby,
garnet, citrine, carnelian and indigo.

## Santa Doesn't Stay

Balance showing love against teaching
everyday drudge and discipline.

Affections are pathways to farewell.
Lose a home and gain a paradigm.

Gifts under the tree remain wrapped
until Santa is a rumor in a sleigh again.

Don't become so lazy that you cannot
find a moment to rest comfortably.

Before getting too deep into a subject,
remember that mastery may be murder.

## Sunday, Waiting for Rain

In the fulness of time, later today,
life will break upon us.
Prophets declared it last night
on the eleven o'clock news.

Those seers implied that seeds
scattered on summer-warmed
soil would soften out to signs
of their destinies, into their

vocations as blades assembled
at suburban castles to keep owners
safe from disparaging remarks
by neighbors and passing drivers.

Salvation will spread a canopy to
overlay hope on scorched
and shriveled specimens a drought
and a water ban brought upon

this realm of comely uniformity.
In predicted release and dramatic
descent, mercy shall fall with evening
on the wilted and the composted.

## Beatitudes

Blessed by their choices
are those who rest near myths
and rarities, by pools of peace

purified in recitation showered
in starlight-rain sent mainly to
the poor, the lost, the lonely,

and the broken-hearted.
Blessed as well are the drifters
and dreamers, watching

from a distance, listening, looking
on, trying to trust apart from
reassurance of examples, finding

faith free of texts in translation,
courage without creeds in recital,
contentment short of signs.

## Finding Time

Jammed at the corner,
we should all be patient
and wait for the light.

We have nowhere to go,
but we cannot wait long
for the light to change,

for a storm to cross over
the Midwest and Upstate
New York, west to east

against the light of the sun,
setting now, warming
a worn-out man standing

alone at the wrong door.
I see him there, across
the street, with next to

nothing in his hands, but
all he needs, waiting
to be welcomed in.

## Notes

Behind “What was Lost Today” is “One Art”, a villanelle by Elizabeth Bishop.

“Borrowers” is based on verse three of “I Sing the Almighty Power of God” by Isaac Watts.

The epigraph to “Night Moves in Paris” is from Psalm 126.

Behind “Oppression” is “A Certain Slant of Light” by Emilie Dickinson.

The epigraph to “Saxonville” is a line from *Celtic Twilight* by William Butler Yeats. The first lines of “Saxonville” refer to Mark 4:12. Saxonville, west of Boston, was a nineteenth century textile mill village. Some of the homes from that time remain beside the road.

The epigraph to “Vernal Song” is a line from a lecture given by Ralph Waldo Emerson in 1841 titled “The Conservative.”

“Pilgrim Moon” was written after the solar eclipse of April 8, 2024.

“Why are You Weeping?” is a meditation on John 20.

“Lost in wonder, love and praise” is the final phrase of the third verse of the hymn “Love Divine, All Loves Excelling” by Charles Wesley. “When the trumpet of the Lord shall sound” is the first line of a hymn by James M. Black.

Some of the poems in this collection were published in earlier versions in *The Examined Life Journal*, *The Ekphrastic Review*, and *Pensive, A Global Journal of Spirituality and the Arts*.

www.ingramcontent.com/pod-product-compliance
Lightning Source LLC
LaVergne TN
LVHW020653100826
845148LV00012B/2466

* 9 7 9 8 3 8 5 2 7 3 4 8 5 *